Animal Body Coverings

Why Do Monkeys and Other Mammals Have Fur?

Holly Beaumont

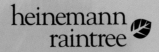

heinemann
raintree

To contact Capstone Global Library please call 800-747-4992, or visit our web site www.capstonepub.com

Edited by Clare Lewis and Kristen Mohn
Designed by Richard Parker
Picture research by Svetlana Zhurkin
Production by Victoria Fitzgerald
Originated by Capstone Global Library
Printed and bound in China by Leo Paper Products Ltd

19 18 17 16 15
10 9 8 7 6 5 4 3 2 1

Library of Congress Cataloging-in-Publication Data
Beaumont, Holly, author.
 Why do monkeys and other mammals have fur? / Holly Beaumont.
   pages cm.—(Animal body coverings)
 Summary: "Find out all about fur and how it helps monkeys keep warm and survive. Discover how fur can be used as camouflage, how fur is different on different mammals and how fur changes as mammals grow up."—Provided by publisher.
 Includes bibliographical references and index.
 ISBN 978-1-4846-2534-7 (hb)—ISBN 978-1-4846-2539-2 (pb)—ISBN 978-1-4846-2549-1 (ebook) 1. Fur—Juvenile literature. 2. Mammals—Juvenile literature. 3. Hair—Juvenile literature. 4. Body covering (Anatomy)—Juvenile literature. 5. Children's questions and answers. I. Title.
 QL942.B43 2016
 599.147—dc23   2015000292

This book has been officially leveled by using the F&P Text Level Gradient™ Leveling System

Acknowledgments
The author and publisher are grateful to the following for permission to reproduce copyright material: Dreamstime: Manit Larpluechai, 19; Getty Images: Visuals Unlimited/Robert Pickett, 20; Minden Pictures: Kevin Schafer, 11; Shutterstock: Alis Leonte, 16, Anan Kaewkhammul, 6 (bottom), Arto Hakola, 10, artpixelgraphy image, 13, Christian Musat, 4, 22 (bottom), Dennis W. Donohue, 6 (middle), EBFoto, 5, 22 (top right), Eduard Kyslynskyy (leopard fur), cover and throughout, Eduardo Rivero, cover (bottom), HHsu, 17, Kongsak Sumano, 12, 23, Lau Chun Kit, 21, Magdanatka, cover (top), Michael Zysman, 7 (middle left), npine, 9, ramarama, 6 (top), 23, Szilvi9, 7 (bottom), TippaPatt, back cover (left), 7 (middle right), Tom Reichner, 14, 23, Traci Law, 18, visceralimage, 8, Yongyut Kumsri, back cover (right), 7 (top), 22 (top left); SuperStock: Biosphoto, 15

We would like to thank Michael Bright for his invaluable help in the preparation of this book.

Contents

Some words are shown in bold, **like this**. You can find them in the picture glossary on page 23.

Which Animals Have Fur?

Mammals have hair or fur.

Mammals are animals that give birth to live young. Mammal mothers make milk to feed their babies.

Different mammals have different types of fur.

Monkeys are mammals. They have fur over almost all of their bodies.

What Is Fur?

Fur is a thick coat of hair that grows over the body.

It is made from the same **material** as your skin and fingernails.

Fur can be long or short.

It can look patterned or plain.

It can feel soft and fluffy or coarse and wiry.

What Is Fur For?

Fur is like a coat or a wool sweater. It helps to keep mammals warm.

Fur traps air next to the animal's skin. This air warms up and keeps the animal warm.

These Japanese macaques live where it is very cold and snowy.

They have long, very thick fur. They can fluff up their fur to trap more air.

Does Fur Keep Mammals Safe?

For animals that live outside all day, fur protects their skin from sunburn.

Fur also protects animals from bites, bumps, and scrapes.

This woolly monkey lives high up in the trees.

Its thick, soft fur protects it from scratches and insect stings.

Does Fur Help Mammals Hide?

Most animals have fur coats that help them blend in with their surroundings.

This tiger's striped fur helps it hide in grass. It can creep up on **prey** without being seen.

This monkey has gray and brown fur.

This helps it to hide in the trees from **predators**.

How Else Can Fur Help Mammals?

Some mammals use their fur to send a message.

When this deer is scared, it flicks its white tail. Other deer see the flash of white and know there's danger.

When this monkey is in danger, its long hair stands on end.

This makes it look bigger and helps scare away an attacker.

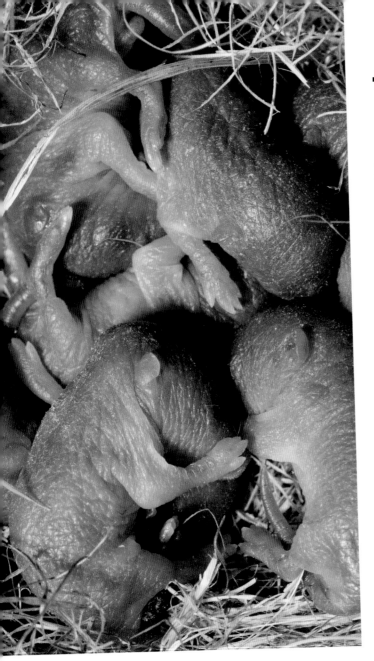

Are Mammals Born with Fur?

Some mammals, including monkeys, are born with thick fur.

Other mammals, like these mice, are born with no fur. Their hair starts to grow when they are a few days old.

Some mammals have only thin fur when they are born.

A mother rabbit pulls fur from her own tummy. She puts this in the nest to help keep her babies warm.

Why Does Some Fur Change Color?

This baby deer has a spotted coat that helps it stay hidden in long grasses.

As it gets older, it will lose its spots and grow a thick new coat for winter.

Leaf monkeys are born with bright orange fur.

This makes it easy for their parents to keep an eye on them.

How Do Mammals Take Care of Their Fur?

It's important for mammals to keep fur free from pests such as fleas.

Fleas are tiny biting bugs. They live and feed on the blood of larger animals, making them weak or sick.

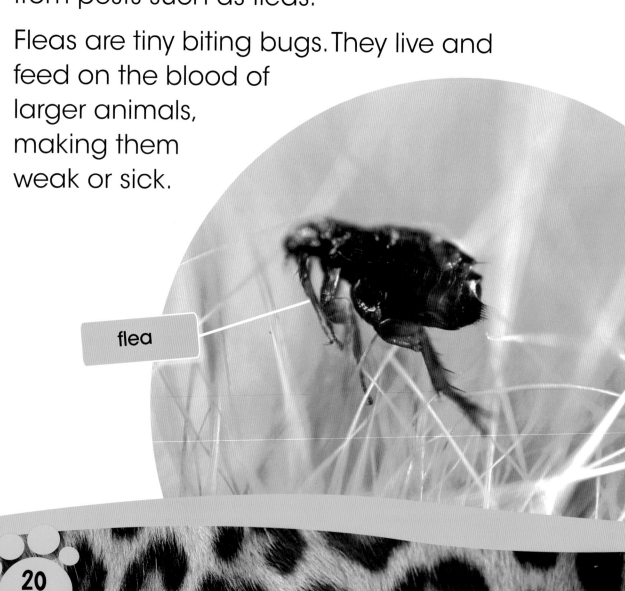

flea

Monkeys check each other's fur for pests. They comb the fur with their fingers.

Monkeys can find it very relaxing!

Fur Quiz

Which of these images shows monkey fur?

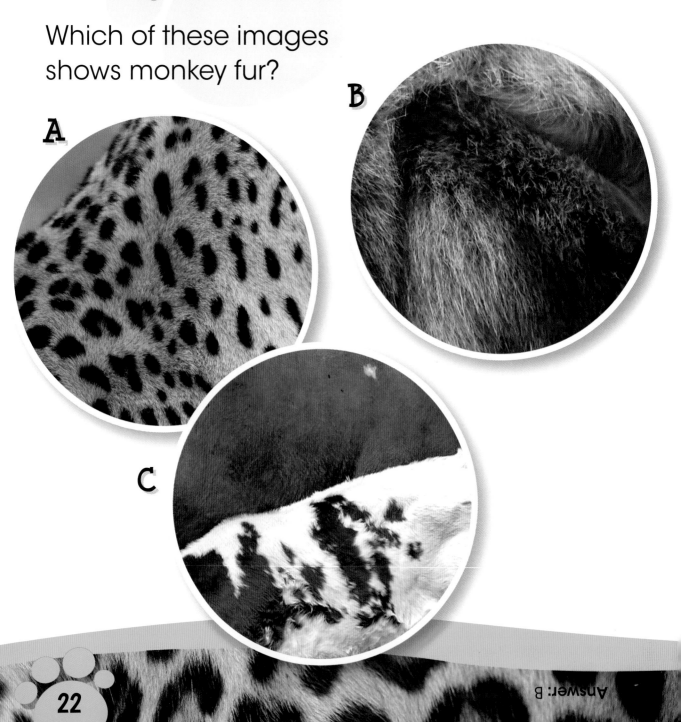

A

B

C

Answer: B

Picture Glossary

 **material** substance from which something is made

 **predator** animal that hunts and eats other animals

 **prey** animal that is hunted and eaten by predators

Find Out More

Web sites

Facthound offers a safe, fun way to find Internet sites related to this book. All of the sites on Facthound have been researched by our staff.

Here's all you do:

Visit *www.facthound.com*

Type in this code: 9781484625347

Books

Boothroyd, Jennifer. *Fur* (Body Coverings). Minneapolis: Lerner, 2012.

Thomas, Isabel. *Marvelous Mammals* (Extreme Animals). Chicago: Raintree, 2013.

Throp, Claire. *Monkeys* (Living in the Wild: Primates). Chicago: Heinemann Library, 2012.

Index